# Al Roker's EXTREME WEATHER

ISBN 978-0-06-248499-4
Typography by Rachel Zegar    17  18  19  20  21  SCP  10  9  8  7  6  5  4  3  2  1    ❖    First Edition

# Al Roker's
# EXTREME WEATHER

AL
ROKER

**HARPER**
*An Imprint of HarperCollinsPublishers*

# CONT

# ENTS

# INTROD

**As a host and weather anchor of the _Today_** show, I fill a lot of roles. I've been to all fifty states, traveled to earthquake and flood zones, and interviewed celebrities from Lin-Manuel Miranda to President Obama. But probably the most important thing I do every day is update viewers about the weather.

Of course, everyone wants to know if they need an umbrella or if it's a good day for the beach—but weather is a lot more complicated than that. It affects everything from school schedules to global transportation, from the

food we eat to the way businesses work. And sometimes, it can mean the difference between life and death.

Extreme weather events such as tornadoes, hurricanes, and blizzards can flatten buildings, disrupt power, and sweep away people caught in their paths.

# UCTION

But with forewarning and planning, people can stay out of harm's way. They can stormproof their homes, stock up on supplies, and move loved ones to safer locations. As a weather anchor, a big part of my job is keeping people informed about dangerous weather events and making sure as many people as possible know how to protect themselves.

I've been forecasting the weather for more than thirty years, and a lot has changed since I started. Forecasters know more about weather events and our climate, we're better at making predictions, and we have a lot more technology and gadgets to use in researching and reporting the weather. But one thing hasn't changed: I love what I do. After you've read this book, I hope you'll understand why.

# PREDICTING

**Predicting the weather is a tricky** business. Global weather is affected by everything from the earth's tilt to **climate change**. Small local systems, such as mountains and lakes, impact air movements and provide moisture to fuel storms.

**Meteorologists** and **hydrologists** use computer programs to decide what the weather is most likely to do next. Scientists know many of the factors that feed extreme weather events. They enter current conditions into computer models to determine how those factors are likely to affect one another.

All of this requires measurements—lots and lots of measurements. In the United States, a government agency called the National Weather Service collects information from weather stations and scientists all over the country. The Storm Prediction Center is responsible for tracking large storms and warning people in their path.

## Time for a Check-up

Just like a doctor uses special tools to find out how your systems are working, meteorologists have equipment that helps them figure out what's going on in the **atmosphere**.

*Satellite images* The National Oceanic and Atmospheric Administration (NOAA) maintains satellites that take images and readings from space. **Polar-orbiting satellites** move around the earth. **Geosynchronous satellites** move at the same speed as the earth so that they are always over the United States. A deep-space satellite gathers information on solar energy from its position a million miles away.

*Doppler radar* sends radio waves toward a storm, where they hit droplets of water, ice, or snow (all forms of **precipitation**) and bounce back. By reading changes in the shape of the radio waves when they return, radar can determine how, and how fast, the storm is moving.

*Weather balloons* carry equipment that measures **temperature**, pressure, and humidity as the balloons rise.

# THE FUTURE

Hurricane Hunter aircraft fly above and directly into hurricanes, dropping special instruments called **dropsondes**. The devices take measurements as they fall, gathering information that helps meteorologists predict the path and intensity of the storm.

To get a complete picture of weather and climate, scientists need data from all over the world. Equipment in weather stations constantly gathers information. But equipment can break down. In remote areas, that means someone needs to stick around to keep things running smoothly. Two engineers staff the Barrow Observatory, at the northernmost point in the United States, year-round.

News of a tornado sends most people scrambling for shelter. But scientists who study them sometimes race toward terrifying tornadoes, trying to gather as much information as they can. This mobile Doppler radar was part of a tornado research project called Vortex 2. It allowed scientists to take close-range readings from the storm.

## What Does Climate Change Have to Do with It?

Your local weather is affected by larger patterns around the world. High in the atmosphere, massive air currents circle the earth. Ocean currents carry warm water from the equator to the poles. Big changes in temperatures, like the ones caused by global climate change, alter air and ocean currents, leading to huge differences in weather patterns, and more extreme weather.

Spider Lightning

# STORMS

With howling winds, lightning, and flash flooding, powerful storms can change a landscape in a matter of minutes. Read on to learn about some of the most dangerous storms—and how to avoid them.

# THUNDERSTORMS

A supercell storm

**Broken trees, downed power lines, flash flooding, and deadly tornadoes—** thunderstorms can mean serious trouble. But they all start with just a little **lift**.

When air temperatures near the ground are much warmer than temperatures higher up, the air is **unstable**. Warm air is less dense than cold air, so a small nudge, called *lift*, will cause the warm air to rise, carrying moisture with it. That moisture reaches colder temperatures in the atmosphere and freezes, forming a cloud of ice crystals. Eventually, the moisture falls as rain, sleet, or hail, bringing cold air down with it. It might sound simple, but that fast-moving cold air can create winds up to one hundred miles per hour, and those ice crystals and changing temperatures can lead to deadly lightning.

In the United States, lightning kills about fifty people every year. Most of those people are caught out in the open, in fields or on the water, when lightning strikes. At the first

## What Is Lightning?

If you've ever gotten a shock from a carpet, you've created lightning. Scuffing picks up extra **electrons** from the carpet and builds up a **negative charge**. Those electrons jump from your finger to a positively charged piece of metal in a bolt of electricity. In a lightning storm, the bolt is much, much bigger, but the story is the same. The thunderstorm clouds carry a big negative charge, and the ground has a **positive charge**. The air between them serves as **insulation**—until the charge becomes too great. Then the electrons jump from one to the other in a supercharged lightning bolt. Lightning can reach 54,000 degrees Fahrenheit. That's almost five times as hot as the sun!

Cloud-to-Ground Lightning

***Cloud-to-ground (CG) lightning*** is a **channel** of electrical current that leaps from a cloud to an object on the ground.

sign of a thunderstorm, the only safe thing to do is head indoors.

Thunderstorms form most often during the summer months. That's when warm, moist air near the ground makes a big storm likely. Occasionally, the conditions necessary for thunder and lightning occur during the winter. Lightning storms during those months are known as **thundersnow**.

## A Bolt from the Blue

Lightning is hot. Really, REALLY hot. As it travels to the ground, it heats the air molecules around it. The superheated molecules explode outward, creating sound waves that we hear as thunder. If you can hear thunder, you are in striking distance—even if the sky above you is blue.

Red sprites

Usually, the electricity in clouds is released as lightning. But sometimes, it produces spectacular effects called **transient luminous events** (TLEs) above the storm. One kind of TLE, called *red sprites*, looks like trailing blobs hovering up to sixty miles above the storm. TLEs are rarely seen from the ground, but have been observed by airplane and space shuttle pilots. These sprites were captured on film by a NASA satellite.

### Intracloud Lightning

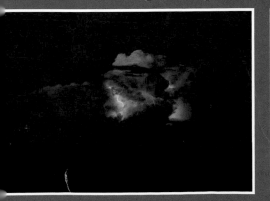

**Intracloud lightning** jumps from one part of a cloud to another, creating a bright flash.

### Cloud Flashes

**Cloud flashes** send channels of electric current out into the air around a cloud but do not connect to the ground.

### Spider Lightning

**Spider lightning** spreads out along the bottom of a cloud.

# TORNADOES

**A single storm system of upward-** flowing warm air (an **updraft**) and downward-flowing cold air (**downdraft**) is called a cell. Single-cell thunderstorms often use up their energy quickly. But sometimes they develop into giant, rotating storms known as *supercells*. Supercells can last for hours, battering the ground with hail, rain, and damaging winds. In the worst-case scenario, the rotating winds of a supercell spawn tornadoes.

A tornado is a column of spinning air that connects a storm cloud to the ground. The top of the column is filled with the same moisture that makes up the cloud, so it appears white. The bottom of the column shreds everything in its path, pummeling trees, buildings, land, and water with winds as fast as 300 miles per hour.

The early stages of a developing tornado, captured in Union City, Oklahoma

## Watch versus Warning

A *tornado watch* means that a tornado has not been spotted yet, but the conditions might lead to twisters. Review safety plans and be ready.

A *tornado warning* means that one has been spotted in the area. Move to a safe place immediately. If you have one, a basement is best. If not, go to a room that does not have windows and does not touch any outside walls.

Fortunately, weather forecasters can spot the conditions that might lead to tornadoes, warning people in time for them to find shelter. Although the United States is struck by about 1,200 tornadoes every year, the number of people killed by them has been dramatically reduced since tornado prediction began in the 1950s.

# Which Twist Is It?

*Supercell tornadoes* grow out of supercell storms. These are often the strongest and most deadly tornadoes.

*Nonsupercell tornadoes* form when rotating air at the ground rises up and reaches a storm cloud.

## Gustnados

*Gustnados* are whirlwinds that develop on the ground and do not reach all the way up to a storm cloud. They rarely grow into full-fledged tornadoes.

Landspouts and waterspouts can be dangerous for people caught in their paths, but they are not usually as strong as supercell tornadoes.

## Landspouts

*Landspouts* form over land. The bottom of the tornado is often the color of the soil or sand it is traveling over.

## Waterspouts

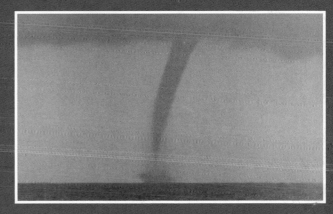

*Waterspouts* form over water.

# How Severe Is It?

Tornadoes are difficult to predict and even harder to measure. Scientists estimate the wind speed of a tornado based on the damage it causes. Since 2007, NOAA has used a number system, called the Enhanced Fujita scale (EF), that looks at damage to trees, buildings, and utility poles to determine a tornado's strength.

| EF | 3-second gust speed |
|---|---|
| 0 | 65–85 mph |
| 1 | 86–110 mph |
| 2 | 111–135 mph |
| 3 | 136–165 mph |
| 4 | 166–200 mph |
| 5 | Over 200 mph |

# DERECHOS
## AND DUST STORMS

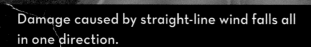

Derecho winds are often found ahead of a line of severe storms, such as this one in central Kansas.

**Have you ever noticed, after a** thunderstorm has passed, that the air is colder than it was before the storm started? Or maybe you've seen, before a storm arrives, trees blowing in the wind.

When rain pours from thunderclouds, it brings cold air down with it. The cold air has to go somewhere, so it moves along the ground, causing wind. The front edge of a storm, where cold air meets warm, is called the **gust** front. A windstorm with gusts faster than 58 miles per hour, and that causes damage along a

Damage caused by straight-line wind falls all in one direction.

## Straight or Swirly?

Because derecho winds tend to go straight, rather than curving, they are known as **straight-line winds**. Both tornado- and straight-line-wind damage can happen in large, powerful thunderstorms. So researchers look at the patterns created by fallen trees and debris to decide whether a tornado has touched down. If trees were knocked over by straight-line winds, they will all be lying in pretty much the same direction. But the spinning winds of a tornado leave trees lying in all different directions.

The circular winds of a tornado leave **debris** in every direction.

line at least 250 miles long, is called a *derecho*. One derecho that struck Kansas, Oklahoma, and Texas in 2001 packed gusts as fast as 100 miles per hour. Winds at that speed can pull shingles and shutters off houses, break branches, and knock out power to homes.

When a windstorm occurs over dry sand or soil, it picks up loose dirt, creating a dust storm or *haboob*. A haboob combines the deadly power of wind with swirling clouds of dust. They are particularly dangerous for drivers.

Not every windstorm is caused by thunderstorm conditions. Chinooks happen in areas near steep mountains. Warm, dry air picks up speed as it blows down along the slope of the mountain and hits the valley with devastating force. One chinook wind that struck Boulder, Colorado, in 1982 damaged 40 percent of the buildings in town. A week later, in the nearby town of Fort Collins, a Chinook wind blew through with gusts up to 140 miles per hour.

Dust storms occur in arid places, where dry conditions lead to powdery sand and soil. Here, a haboob moves across the Moroccan desert.

## What Is Wind Speed, Anyway?

A car traveling down the highway can maintain the exact same speed for a long period of time, so it's easy to say how fast it is going. But wind rarely travels at a steady rate. To help give a better picture of what conditions are really like in a storm, meteorologists measure a few different kinds of speed.

**Gust speed** is the fastest speed measured. Depending on the situation, this speed might need to last for several seconds, or for as little as one.

**Sustained wind speed** is an average of speeds recorded over a period of two minutes.

**Maximum sustained wind** is the highest wind speed that lasts for at least one minute.

# HAILSTORMS

Hailstones can range from tiny round pebbles to giant baseball-size hunks.

**What happens when the ice** crystals in clouds fall to the earth? Most of the time, they melt before they reach the ground, turning into rain. But if storm conditions are just right, the crystals turn into hail.

Remember all that rising air carrying moisture from the ground up to thunderstorm clouds? Sometimes, that **updraft** is strong enough to hold ice up in the colder zones of the atmosphere. It may begin to fall before being blown back up, or it may simply remain in the cloud, where it comes into contact with supercooled water. Supercooled water is still liquid, even though it is colder than 32 degrees Fahrenheit. When it touches ice, it freezes onto it, creating a hailstone that grows larger and larger. Chunks of ice can also collide and freeze together. When the hailstones finally fall, they're big enough to reach the ground before melting away.

Hail falls in the summer, when thunderstorm conditions are common. It isn't usually dangerous to people. But hailstorms do cause a lot of damage, destroying crops and denting cars and house roofs. Being hit by a piece of ice isn't that different from getting clocked by a stone, so take shelter if you notice hailstones.

Large hail can do damage to buildings, knocking loose roof tiles, breaking windows, and shredding siding.

Hailstones litter a high mountainside.

## Hailstone Alley

Although hail can occur anywhere, it's more likely to fall in areas that are high up, like the Rocky Mountains. That's because high elevations are closer to the cold layers of the atmosphere where ice forms. Hailstones have a shorter distance to fall to the ground, and are less likely to melt completely before they get there. The High Plains of the United States get more hail than the rest of the country. "Hailstone Alley," where Nebraska, Colorado, and Wyoming meet, averages seven to nine hail days a year.

Scientists aren't sure why, but hail and tornadoes often go hand in hand. Hail can occur without tornadoes. But the same storm conditions that spawn twisters usually create hail, too. Storm chasers look for hail in a thunderstorm as one of the first signs that tornadoes may be coming. The windshield of this research vehicle was shattered by hail as meteorologists pursued a tornado.

Large hail smashed the windshield of this tornado-chasing vehicle from the National Severe Storms laboratory.

# WINTER STORMS

Slippery roadways make driving during winter storms dangerous.

**Just like summer storms, winter storms** occur when lift carries moisture to the clouds. And also like summer storms, winter storms can be extremely dangerous for people caught unaware.

In the cold zones of the upper atmosphere, water droplets form into ice crystals. Whether those crystals fall to the ground as snow, ice, or rain depends on the temperature of the atmospheric layers below a cloud. If all of the air below the cloud is warmer than 32 degrees Fahrenheit, the ice crystals melt and fall to the ground as raindrops. But if all of the air below the cloud is below freezing (32 degrees Fahrenheit), more moisture will freeze onto the ice crystal, creating snow. Snowstorms dump snow on sidewalks, roads, and building roofs. All of that extra weight can mean trouble for houses and other buildings with weak structures. Branches and power lines often come down in snowstorms, too.

When falling ice crystals travel through a thin band of warm air before reaching freezing temperatures on the ground, they may melt into large water droplets—then freeze again to become sleet. Sleet reaches the ground as tiny round pieces of ice.

And if that band of warm air is wider, it can create the slipperiest conditions of all: freezing rain. Freezing rain occurs when the ice crystals melt, but do not have time to refreeze into ice. Instead, they hit the ground as supercooled water, which instantaneously freezes onto anything it

The perfectly symmetrical, six-sided shape that many people call a snowflake is actually a snow crystal—a single ice crystal whose exact shape depends on the different temperatures that it passes through as it is forming. As the snow crystals fall, they often combine with others, making the larger, fluffy structures that are referred to as snowflakes.

## No-Snow Blizzards

When winds reach 35 miles per hour, conditions are ripe for a **blizzard**. Blizzards often happen when high winds accompany snowstorms. But they can occur without snowfall.

In a *ground blizzard*, loose snow that is already on the ground is lifted up and blown around. These are blizzard conditions—even if no snow is falling from the sky.

## Lake-Effect Storms

Areas surrounding the Great Lakes can get epic snowstorms known as lake-effect storms. Because the water of the lakes is warmer than the air, cold wind blowing across the lakes causes water to evaporate and rise. The Great Lakes are big—REALLY big—and that means there's a lot of water to evaporate. When the cold winds reach the shore, all of that moisture comes down as snow.

touches—an ice storm! Brittle tree branches, groaning under the weight of the ice, can snap, downing power lines and creating a hazard for anyone nearby.

Ice storms and snowstorms are a hazard for drivers, and most winter storm deaths are caused by car accidents on roads that are slippery. And all of those falling branches and power lines can leave people without heat when temperatures are well below freezing. When winter storms are coming, it's best to stock up on supplies and get ready to stay home—and stay warm—for up to three days.

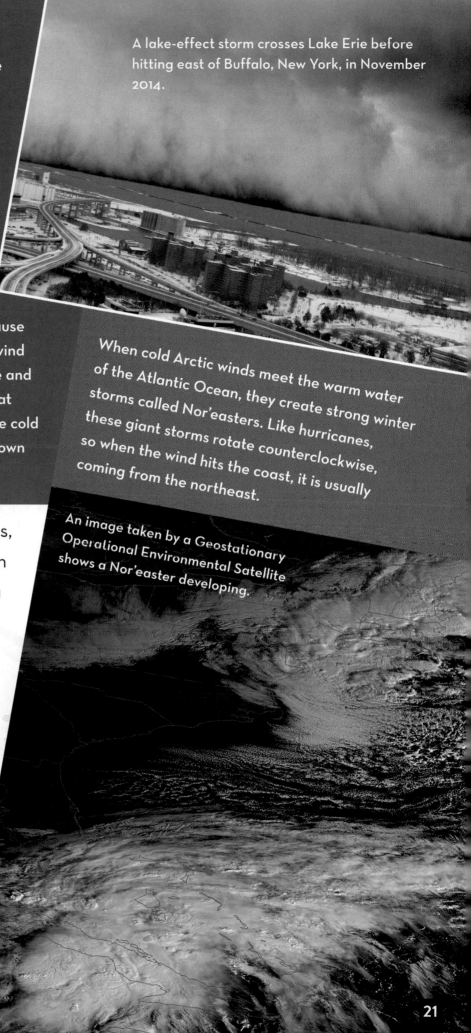

A lake-effect storm crosses Lake Erie before hitting east of Buffalo, New York, in November 2014.

When cold Arctic winds meet the warm water of the Atlantic Ocean, they create strong winter storms called Nor'easters. Like hurricanes, these giant storms rotate counterclockwise, so when the wind hits the coast, it is usually coming from the northeast.

An image taken by a Geostationary Operational Environmental Satellite shows a Nor'easter developing.

# TROPICAL CYCLONES

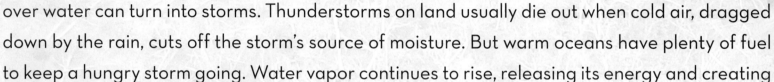

**Warm ocean waters might be perfect for surfing and** snorkeling, but they can also spawn the world's most destructive storms: tropical cyclones. When ocean temperatures reach 80 degrees Fahrenheit and tropical winds blow, water from the ocean's surface evaporates and rises to form clouds. Just like they do over land, rising air and moisture over water can turn into storms. Thunderstorms on land usually die out when cold air, dragged down by the rain, cuts off the storm's source of moisture. But warm oceans have plenty of fuel to keep a hungry storm going. Water vapor continues to rise, releasing its energy and creating strong winds. Tropical cyclones are usually about 50,000 feet high and 125 miles across, and pack winds traveling more than 74 miles per hour. The strongest storms blow

## Categorizing the Wind

Scientists track tropical cyclones closely, using radar, satellite images, and measurements taken by hurricane-hunting aircraft to determine how dangerous a storm is. They use a special system called the Saffir–Simpson scale to rate the strength of the storm.

|  | WIND SPEED (MPH) | IMPACT |
| --- | --- | --- |
| Category 1 | 74–95 | Very dangerous winds, some damage |
| Category 2 | 96–110 | Extremely dangerous winds, extensive damage |
| Category 3 | 111–129 | Devastating damage |
| Category 4 | 130–156 | Catastrophic damage |
| Category 5 | 157 or higher | Catastrophic damage; a high percentage of houses will be destroyed |

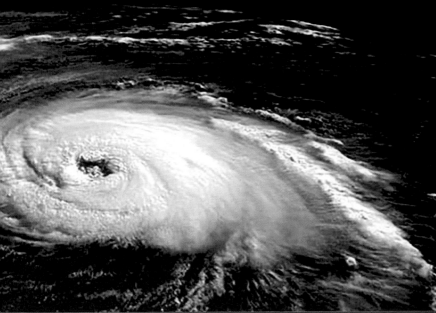

This photo of Hurricane Isabel was taken by a satellite in September 2003.

## Corio-WHAT?

From space, a tropical cyclone looks like a pinwheel with a hole called the **eye** at the center, and curved arms extending outward. In the Northern Hemisphere, tropical cyclones rotate in a counterclockwise direction. In the Southern Hemisphere, they rotate clockwise. Why do they whirl? Because the earth is a spinning globe, places near the equator are traveling through space faster than places that are closer to the poles. The differences in speed cause the wind to arc as it travels away from the equator. This is called the *Coriolis effect*.

at more than 150 miles per hour.

Tropical cyclones that form in the Atlantic and northeast Pacific Oceans are called *hurricanes*. In the northwest Pacific, they are called *typhoons*, and in the southern Pacific and Indian oceans they are simply referred to as *cyclones*.

No matter what they're called, tropical cyclones can spell trouble for people who live near the oceans where they form.

Punishing winds can lift roofs off houses and demolish walls. But much of the damage from a tropical cyclone is caused by **storm surge**—strong, high waves that pummel the shoreline, flattening everything in their path. The most deadly natural disaster in American history was a hurricane that hit Galveston, Texas, in 1900. Fifteen-foot waves swept over the island, pushing demolished homes and broken trees inland, and killing more than 8,000 people. Today, seawalls protect Galveston from rising waters, and scientists are better at predicting dangerous storms. They can issue hurricane warnings to people in harm's way, giving them time to **evacuate** to safety.

Homes flattened by storm surge caused by the Galveston hurricane of 1900

Hardpan is created by extended drought.

# DANGEROUS CONDITIONS

They may not be as dramatic as hurricanes and tornadoes, but cold, heat, drought, and fog kill more people in the United States than the worst storms. Keep reading to learn what you should do if you find yourself in one of these deadly situations.

# DROUGHT

Following several years of drought, this lake in California had receded to a fraction of its original size in 2014.

**Water is essential to our lives.** We use it for cooking, bathing, drinking, and washing. Water is also necessary for agriculture. Without it, plants won't grow, and without food crops, there is nothing to eat.

When rain falls, or snow melts, some of the water runs off into rivers and streams, where it will eventually flow to lakes and oceans. Some of the water soaks into the soil, where thirsty plants use it up, and some of it trickles down through the tiny spaces between rocks and dirt, to join groundwater, which is stored in aquifers deep under the earth.

A drought occurs when there is not enough rain and snow for a long period of time. Droughts are a normal part of the weather cycle. But droughts that last for a very long time can bring water reserves to dangerous lows, imperiling drinking-water supplies and farming.

When there is not enough readily accessible water in

In the 1930s, several states in the Great Plains suffered through a massive drought, which lasted as long as eight years in some places. An unusual lack of rainfall in an already dry area was made worse by the fact that farmers had plowed over tough, deep-rooted prairie grass in order to plant crops. When those crops died due to lack of water, they left dry, bare soil exposed to the wind. Strong winds kicked up enormous dust storms, and the hard-hit area, covering about 150,000 square miles in Texas, Oklahoma, Kansas, Colorado, and New Mexico, became known as the Dust Bowl.

## Going, Going, Gone

Aquifers are pockets of water stored in rock that is full of tiny holes, like a sponge, or in larger chambers between layers of nonporous rock. Aquifers hold much of the world's drinkable water. In the United States, about 33 percent of the water supplied by towns and cities, and 97 percent of the water for homes in rural areas, comes from underground aquifers. The High Plains Aquifer, also known as the Ogallala Aquifer, runs under the central United States, covering 174,000 square miles and providing most of the water for farming in the region.

*Aquifers* are hidden deep under the soil, so how can we tell how much water is in them? Scientists

An artist's rendering of a GRACE satellite in orbit

working on NASA's Gravity Recovery and Climate Experiment (GRACE) calculate the amount of groundwater hidden beneath the earth's surface by measuring tiny changes in the orbits of two satellites. By figuring out how the pull of gravity changes as the satellites pass over certain areas, the scientists can measure differences in the amount of water stored there.

lakes and **reservoirs**, dry regions often turn to groundwater to make up the difference. And groundwater is replaced more slowly in areas experiencing a drought. Of the 37 largest aquifers in the world, 13 are significantly stressed, with people using far more water than can be replenished. Once those stores are gone, it could be hundreds of years before they are refilled by rain and melted snow.

Water held in reservoirs and ponds dwindles during droughts.

## Turn Off the Tap!

As with most natural resources, everyone shares groundwater. When drought affects the amount of water entering the groundwater system, it lowers the level of the water for everyone. Here are a few simple things that you can do to save water:

- Turn off the faucet while you are brushing your teeth.
- Don't run your laundry or dishwasher until you have a full load.
- Check for leaks around your house, especially dripping faucets, and let an adult know that they need to be fixed.
- If you take baths, fill the bathtub halfway instead of to the top. If you take showers, time yourself. Shorter showers mean less water use.

# FOG

If you live anywhere near mountains or a body of water, chances are that you've woken up to some foggy mornings. A thick cloud of moist air, fog forms over lakes and oceans, in mountain valleys, and anywhere else that cool air at the ground level combines with a lot of suspended moisture.

The amount of water that air can hold (the relative humidity) changes with the temperature. Warm air can hold a lot of moisture. Cold air can hold far less. If there is more moisture in the air than it can hold, the humidity has reached the saturation point. Water vapor will begin to form into droplets and fall out of the air.

Advection fog surrounds the Golden Gate Bridge in San Francisco, California.

## Frozen Fogsicles

If fog forms when the air is below the freezing temperature, it may freeze onto plants and objects it comes in contact with, creating a beautiful, but dangerously slippery, ice shell.

### Advection fog

**Advection fog** occurs when moist air is cooled by contact with the ground. When it cools enough that it can no longer hold water vapor, fog is created. Lake and sea fog are examples of advection fog.

In fog conditions, the air near the ground (or a body of water) is colder than the air above it. Moisture in this air can no longer be held as vapor, so it condenses into a cloud of water droplets.

Fog can make it difficult to see. Drivers can lose track of the road and other cars, boaters may not be able to see navigation buoys, and pilots can have a hard time finding landing strips—and even avoiding mountaintops.

Fog generally appears in the early morning, when changing temperatures can lead to big differences between the ground and the air. It disappears as the sun warms the air later in the day, turning all of those tiny drops of water back into an invisible vapor.

When dense fog covers roadways, experts say that drivers should turn off their high beams and use low beams or fog lights instead. That's because the millions of tiny water droplets in the air act like tiny reflectors, shining light back. When that light hits your eye, it makes it difficult to see, much like bright sun glare can make it hard to see during the day.

## Radiation fog

*Radiation fog* occurs as moist air near the ground cools overnight. Without sun to warm the ground, the ground releases heat into the layers near it. As the lower levels of air cool, the water condenses. Mountain valley fog is an example of radiation fog.

## Evaporation fog

*Evaporation fog*, also called steam fog, occurs when moisture evaporates off warmer water into cold air. Evaporation fog sometimes causes wispy trails of fog off streams and lakes.

# EXTREME HEAT

**Hurricanes and tornadoes blow with dev-** astating force. Lightning storms rattle windows with driving rain and thunder. Yet, in the United States, more people are killed by extreme heat every year— about 124—than by any other weather disaster.

In typical weather, the earth absorbs **thermal energy** (heat) from the sun during the day, which makes the ground warmer. The ground then warms the air closest to it, and the air rises toward lower pressure areas higher up in the atmosphere. At night, there is no energy from the sun for the earth to absorb, but the air warmed during the day continues to rise, cooling things down.

But when areas of higher pressure appear in the atmosphere above, there's nowhere for the rising warm air to go. It bumps into the **high-pressure zone** and turns back toward the earth, becoming trapped below a high-pressure "lid." Temperatures grow hotter and hotter.

When the heat climbs out of the usual range for an area, electrical grids become stressed by the energy demands of millions of air conditioners and fans. In areas where they're rarely needed, people might not have air conditioners and fans at all. And that can spell trouble.

## What's the Big Deal?

When temperatures start to rise, blood vessels in our skin **dilate**, or get bigger, releasing heat from our bodies into the air. But if the air temperature gets hotter than our body temperature, there's no place for that heat to go. That's when sweat comes in. Sweat cools us off through **evaporation**. The water molecules absorb heat and begin to move, eventually losing their grip on each other and drifting off into the air, taking the energy with them. But too much sweating means that your body is losing a lot of water and important **minerals**. And if it is too hot for sweat to be effective, people can suffer from dangerous conditions such as **heat exhaustion** and **heatstroke**.

People flock to pools and beaches to cool off in hot weather.

A NOAA weather map shows the effects of a heat dome across the United States.

WPC DAY 3 MAX T TMP FCST
ISSUED: 14112 THU 21 2016
VALID: SUN 24 JUL 2016
FORECASTER: FOCCIN
DOC/NOAA/NWS/NCEP/WPC

30  35  40  45  50  55  60  65  70  75  80  85  90  95  100  105

## It's All Relative

Temperature alone doesn't always indicate how hot you feel on a summer day, because humidity affects how good you are at cooling off. Sweat cools things down through evaporation, but in order for the water in your sweat to evaporate, there needs to be somewhere for it to go. There's water **vapor** in most air, but how much can vary a lot. The amount of water vapor in the air is called **humidity**. When humidity levels are high, evaporation is slower. That means that our bodies have a harder time cooling off. So even if the actual temperature is 98 degrees Fahrenheit, on a very humid day it might feel like it's 105 degrees. Meteorologists use the **heat index** to give you a sense of how hot it really feels outside.

It's important to drink enough water to help your body stay hydrated in the heat.

31

# EXTREME COLD

**No matter where you live, tem**-peratures are always colder in the winter and warmer in the summer. Exactly how cold and warm they get depends on where your home is on the globe. In general, places closer to the equator enjoy warmer winters and endure sweltering summers. Places closer to the poles shiver in the winter, and have cooler summers.

In the Northern Hemisphere, however, shifts in the jet stream can have a dramatic effect on exactly how cold things get in the winter. That's because the jet stream corrals an area of very cold air and high pressure, called the polar vortex, around the North Pole. Differences between the low pressure of the vortex and

## Bundle Up

In cold weather, your body has to work to keep you warm. Blood vessels near the skin constrict, or become smaller, so that less heat will be lost. Your body also changes the way that it uses energy, burning calories to release heat into your body. If temperatures get too cold, you start to shiver—your muscles contract and rattle, creating even more heat. But sometimes that isn't enough. If fingers, noses, and toes become too cold, parts of them can freeze, a condition called **frostbite**. In the worst cases, frostbite leads to gangrene, a condition in which the tissues die. If your body can't keep itself warm enough on the inside, it is called **hypothermia**. Hypothermia can be life-threatening. It's important to stay warm and dry, wearing appropriate clothes and staying out of extreme cold as much as possible.

higher pressure farther south fuel the strong winds of the jet stream, which hold all of that cold air in place. When temperatures around the pole are warmer than usual, there isn't as much difference in pressure between the two zones, and that weakens the jet stream, which can cause it to move. When that happens, the polar vortex reaches farther south, bringing its freezing temperatures down into North America.

It's not just people and animals who have to look out for extreme cold. Plants and trees suffer, too. In Florida, citrus fruits, including grapefruits and oranges, are an important crop. If temperatures dip below freezing (32 degrees Fahrenheit), the fruit can freeze on the trees. Even in northern climates, where fruit is not growing during the winter, a late cold snap can still threaten fruit harvests by damaging tree buds in the spring.

Citrus growers protect their fruit from freezing by spraying water on the plants. As the water freezes, it releases energy into the oranges, protecting them from damage. Here, water sprayed on citrus trees is melting as temperatures warm.

## Keeping It Chill

Your body is great at maintaining a steady internal temperature. But some heat is lost through your skin—especially when cold winds blow. The average internal body temperature hovers around 98.6 degrees Fahrenheit, but the skin on your face varies from about 90 to 93 degrees Fahrenheit. If air temperatures around you are cooler, your skin warms the air next to it. When wind passes over your skin it displaces, or pushes away, that warmer air, leaving more cool air next to your skin. So you lose more heat as you warm that fresh, cooler air. Wind also causes moisture in the skin to evaporate, causing even more heat loss. That means on a day when the temperature is thirty-five degrees Fahrenheit, a ten-mile-per-hour wind can make it feel like twenty-seven degrees. Meteorologists look at air temperature and wind speeds to figure out the **wind chill,** which gives a better sense of what outside temperatures will feel like.

Snow tumbles down a rocky slope
in the Caucasus Mountains.

# AFTERMATH

After the heat or the snow, the rain and the wind, the worst may be yet to come. Devastating effects of extreme weather can strike suddenly, long after the initial danger has passed.

# FLOODS

**When it rains, it pours. When it** snows, it pours. When hurricanes blow, it pours—water, that is. Storms and rainfall dump water on the landscape year in and year out. In warm weather, water falls as rain or hail. Water that fell as snow and sleet in cold weather melts and turns back into water in the spring.

In the end, all that water has to go somewhere. Most of it runs into streams and rivers, which eventually make their way to lakes and the ocean. A lot of it is absorbed into the soil, where it trickles down to replenish groundwater.

On average, about 82 people are killed by floods in the United States each year. More than half of those deaths are caused by people driving into **floodwaters**. Others are killed when they wade in. Just six inches of water is enough to sweep adults off their feet. Twelve inches can carry away a car. The most important rule in a flood is—don't go in!

The streets of New Orleans were flooded during Hurricane Katrina in 2005.

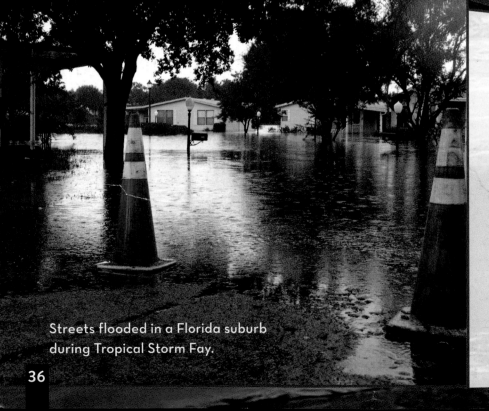

Streets flooded in a Florida suburb during Tropical Storm Fay.

In years of heavy precipitation, when there's more than water systems can handle, flooding occurs. Spilling out of rivers and storm drains and overrunning levees, water can scour the landscape and demolish structures. Water moves with devastating force. One **cubic yard** of water (about half the size of a refrigerator box) weighs almost 1,700 pounds.

# Types of Floods

### Flash floods

### River floods

### Storm surge

***Flash floods*** can turn a dry riverbed (often referred to as a dry wash) into a raging flood in a matter of minutes. Flash floods happen when water rushes down slopes and comes together in one channel. They are common in river- and streambeds, canyons, and man-made channels, such as roads. Canyon flooding can be particularly dangerous, as it can channel water from storms happening miles away and catch people by surprise.

***River floods*** happen when water runs over the banks of a river. Often, this occurs with unusually large rains or melting snow, but can also be the result of river damming by storm debris or ice.

***Storm surge*** is an unusually high tide that rushes ashore during severe storms. Storm surge is the most deadly factor in massive storms like tropical cyclones and nor'easters.

When Hurricane Katrina struck the Gulf Coast of the United States in August 2005, it became the most destructive hurricane in American history, causing more than $100 billion in damage. While the storm grazed the southern tip of Florida and struck both Louisiana and Mississippi, most of the damage occurred in New Orleans, where flooding destroyed much of the city. Parts of New Orleans are as much as eight feet below **sea level.** Seawalls and levees (artificial banks of land designed to hold back water) protect the city from the waters that surround it, but during the hurricane, storm surge overtook the levees and rushed into the city. About 1,200 people were killed by Hurricane Katrina and the flooding that followed.

When levees failed in New Orleans following Hurricane Katrina, some neighborhoods were completely submerged.

Storm surge flattened thousands of trees in Slidell, Louisiana, in 2005.

# WILDFIRES

**During dry or exceptionally hot** weather, wildfires (also called **wildland** fires) break out. Every year, wildfires consume millions of acres of land in the United States—in 2015, more than 10 million acres burned. Like all fires, wildfires need three conditions, known as the *fire triangle*, to burn: fuel, **oxygen,** and heat (or a spark). Up to 90 percent of wildfires may be started by humans, but the other 10 percent are started by the weather, mostly in the form of lightning.

A plane drops flame retardant on a wildfire in New Mexico in 2011.

Putting out wildfires is a tricky and dangerous business. Airplanes and helicopters can drop water from the sky, but that only slows the fire down and lowers temperatures so that firefighters can move in. The surest way to stop a blaze is to deprive it of fuel. Firefighters can do this in a number of ways. They start smaller, controlled burns ahead of the fire's path to eat up the fuel before the big fire arrives, knock down and clear out low brush, and dig deep trenches to stop the spread of ground fires.

Wildfires can burn and spread in different ways. Depending on the fuel available, a wildfire might pack one or two of these types of flames—or all three.

### Ground fires

*Ground fires* burn beneath the surface, eating up plant matter in the soil.

### Surface fires

*Surface fires* produce flames as they burn fuel, such as dried leaves and branches, on the ground.

### Crown fires

*Crown fires* spread in the tree canopy, burning leaves and branches that are high on the trees.

Once a fire is set, it also needs weather to help it along. Dry branches and leaf litter make perfect fuel for a fire, so wildfires blaze out of control in dry seasons, or as a result of drought. The flames burn along the ground and leap from tree to tree, fed by winds that deliver oxygen and blow sparks to new locations.

Wildfires are a serious danger to homes and people—a typical wildfire has flames about three feet high, and temperatures up to 1,500 degrees Fahrenheit. The only way to put out a wildfire is to break the triangle. Firefighters dig ditches and clear brush to deprive the fire of fuel. And, of course, weather sometimes provides the best solution: prolonged rain makes fuel damp, lowers temperatures, and smothers coals, knocking out the most stubborn fires.

## Considering Climate Change

Over the past decades, the number of wildfires every year has increased. As climate change shifts rain and snow patterns, it also affects the length of wildfire seasons. In the west, snowmelt provides much of the moisture. Snow builds up in the mountains over the winter, then melts and trickles down into the foothills and flatlands in the spring. Climate change is shortening the snow season, resulting in earlier snowmelt and less snow overall. That means a longer, drier summer—and more wildfires.

Wildland firefighters use shovels and chainsaws to isolate fires and put them out.

Wildfires spread faster and burn hotter over mountainous terrain, and that means that the nastiest fires burn in hard-to-reach places. Hotshots are highly trained wilderness firefighters who work in teams, flying into remote areas under some of the most dangerous and uncomfortable conditions. To be a Hotshot, a firefighter needs to be in great physical shape, trained in wilderness survival and firefighting, and willing to fly anywhere to spend days in the woods on a moment's notice.

# LANDSLIDES

**While downed trees and crumbled houses** are more obvious, big storms and fires can also cause problems where you may not think to look—below the soil. Landslides are giant cascades of boulders, rocks, loose dirt, mud, or other debris that come tumbling down hillsides when the structures that hold them up have been damaged.

Heavy rains can eat away at the soil that supports rocks and trees, eventually leading to their collapse. When the force of gravity pushing down on rocks on a hillside becomes stronger than the support beneath them, they begin to slide. *Landslides* can move slowly, creeping downhill by mere inches a year. Or they can rip downhill at breakneck speeds of up to 200 miles per hour.

Mount Saint Helens erupts on July 22, 1980.

Landslides are often triggered by the powerful tremors associated with earthquakes and volcanic eruptions. When Mount Saint Helens, in Washington State, erupted in 1980, it sent 0.6 cubic miles of material—enough to fill 1 million Olympic-size swimming pools—down the sides of the mountain at speeds as fast as 150 miles per hour. It was the largest landslide in recorded history.

A steam blast from the Mount Saint Helens crater, April 6, 1980

# Going with the Flow

Because of their steep slopes, loose surfaces, and tendency to rumble, volcanoes are common sites for landslides.

## Pyroclastic Flows

## Lahars

*Pyroclastic flows* carry hot ash, rock, and gas downhill during volcanic eruptions at speeds of up to 150 miles per hour. Temperatures in a pyroclastic flow can be as hot as 1,500 degrees Fahrenheit.

*Lahars* are mudflows that carry volcanic material, mud, and water down the steep slopes of volcanoes. Homes downhill can become completely buried in mud.

When heavy rainfall hits soil that is already holding a lot of water, the water can sluice down slopes and into valleys, carrying along debris, soil, and rocks in its path. Mudslides, also called debris flows, can be extremely dangerous to people and homes downhill, as they move very quickly and often without warning, burying every-thing in their paths.

Trees and other deep-rooted plants are the best defense against mud and soil slides, since roots hold soil in place. Hills are more likely to suffer mudslides in the years after a wildfire has damaged anchoring plants. The heat of wildfires can also change the surface of soil, making it harder and less absorbent (called hard-pan). That means more water remains at the surface to run off and cause trouble for those downhill.

A lahar engulfs a neighborhood following an eruption of Mount Pinatubo in the Philippines.

# AVALANCHES

**Have you ever wondered why** mountain peaks are so often covered in snow? As air moves along the terrain, it has to flow up the slopes of mountains. Air tends to get colder the higher up you go—about 3.5 degrees Fahrenheit for every 1,000 feet of **altitude**. So as the air rises, it cools. Moisture in the air turns into ice crystals and dumps snow on high peaks.

The colder temperatures on the top of the mountain mean that all of that snow is likely to stick around for a while. It builds up in layers, each one reflecting the different characteristics of the snowfall that caused it. Some layers are fluffy and loose, some wet and dense, some thick, and some thin.

Warming temperatures, blowing wind, or human activity can bring all of that snow down the mountainside in a fast-moving slide.

An avalanche can overtake people downhill, leaving them trapped. About 25 people—mostly snowshoers, skiers, snowmobilers, and snowboarders—are killed by avalanches in the United States every year.

## Snow Avalanches

When loose snow tumbles down a mountain slope, picking up more snow as it goes, it is called a *loose snow avalanche*. Loose snow avalanches don't usually cause much damage to buildings, but they may sweep people up.

## Slab Avalanches

When an entire chunk of packed snow breaks loose and slides downhill, it is called a *slab avalanche*. Slab avalanches will carry away anyone caught in their path, and can flatten buildings as well.

## Silly Name, Serious Danger

When is a "whumpf" not funny? When it means an avalanche is possible! If a skier or snowmobiler is caught in an avalanche, odds are high that it was caused by humans. According to NOAA, 90 percent of avalanche incidents are caused by the victim or by someone who was with them. Moving on top of unstable snow can collapse hidden layers underneath it, making a distinct "whumpf" sound. People who spend time in avalanche zones should be aware of warning signs an avalanche may be coming.

Check the slope. Avalanches occur on hills that have more than a thirty-degree slope.

Pay attention to the snow. Cracks in the snow and signs of an earlier avalanche are good indications that an avalanche may occur. You may also hear "whumpfing," a sound below your feet made by snow collapsing under you.

Look for triggers. Avalanches can be caused by people on the slope above, or by high winds, new snow, or changing temperatures.

# THE FINAL WORD

**Extreme weather can be terrifying** and fascinating. But earthquakes, mudslides, heat waves, and hurricanes are just the tip of the iceberg. Every day, weather affects our lives in a thousand small ways, and some pretty big ones, too! Those ways are changing as man-made global warming alters temperatures and weather systems around the world. And that means there's never been a more exciting time to learn about the weather.

Scientists discover new things about our climate every day. And as it's changing, you can learn more, too. Read the news to find out about extreme weather events as they occur around the world, check in with the local weather to find out what's happening in your area, and visit some of the great websites on page forty-seven to learn more about both.

Best of all, you can share what you've learned. Spread the word about weather and climate change. Let your friends and neighbors know how they can prepare for changes in the weather, and what to do when extreme weather hits. You can be the weather anchor of your family and help share the surprising, scary, amazing, and beautiful world of weather.

# BIGGEST, DEADLIEST, MOST EXTREME

## DEADLIEST TORNADO

On March 18, 1925, the Tri-State Tornado traveled 219 miles from Missouri to Indiana, killing 695 people and injuring 2,027.

## FASTEST WIND GUST SPEED

The fastest wind gust speed ever recorded was measured on Barrow Island, off the coast of Australia, in 1996. That year, Tropical Cyclone Olivia blew through with a maximum gust speed of 253 miles per hour.

## HIGHEST TEMPERATURE

The highest confirmed temperature measured on earth was 134 degrees Fahrenheit, recorded in Death Valley, California, on July 10, 1913.

## LOWEST TEMPERATURE

The coldest temperature measured on earth was -135.8 degrees Fahrenheit, recorded by a NASA satellite between Dome Argue and Dome Fuji on the Antarctic ice sheet on August 10, 2010.

## DEADLIEST HURRICANE

Although it's difficult to pin down an exact toll, the Galveston hurricane of 1900 remains the deadliest hurricane on record with more than 8,000 killed. The next deadliest hurricane, which struck southeast Florida in 1928, killed between 2,500 and 3,000 people.

## COSTLIEST HURRICANE

Hurricane Katrina, which struck Florida, Louisiana, Alabama, and Mississippi in 2005, caused more property damage than any other hurricane to date, costing about $108 billion.

## DEADLIEST FOG

From December 5–9, 1952, a heavy mixture of smoke and fog (also called smog) formed in the city of London. More than 4,000 died as a result of what became known as the Great Smog.

## DEADLIEST FLOOD IN THE UNITED STATES

On May 31, 1889, a dam in Johnstown, Pennsylvania, broke after two days of heavy rain. Twenty million gallons of water rushed into the valley below, killing 2,209 people.

## BIGGEST LANDSLIDE

The largest landslide recorded on earth occurred during the eruption of Mount Saint Helens on May 18, 1980. More than 3.6 billion cubic yards of soil, rock, and ash slid downhill.

## LARGEST HAILSTONE IN THE UNITED STATES

The largest hailstone recorded in the United States fell in Vivian, South Dakota, on July 23, 2010. It was eight inches across and weighed almost two pounds.

# GLOSSARY

**air pressure.** The force created by air molecules pressing against a surface.

**altitude.** A measure of how high something is compared to the sea level.

**aquifer.** A layer of rock that is filled with tiny holes that store water underground.

**atmosphere.** The envelope of gases that surrounds the earth.

**channel.** A narrow passage through which something (such as water or electricity) flows.

**climate change.** Changes to the large weather systems on the earth caused by the addition of human-made gases to the atmosphere.

**cubic yard.** An area that is three feet wide, three feet high, and three feet deep.

**debris.** Pieces left behind after something has broken apart. In nature, debris often includes broken branches and fallen trees.

**dilate.** To grow wider or bigger.

**Doppler radar.** A type of radar that bounces radio waves off an object and measures changes in the signal to determine how fast the object is moving.

**dropsonde.** A special instrument that is designed to be dropped from an aircraft, take measurements as it falls, and radio back information before it reaches the ground.

**electrons.** Tiny particles that orbit the center of an atom and provide a negative charge.

**evacuate.** To leave an area in order to escape danger.

**evaporation.** The process by which molecules in a liquid break apart to become a gas.

**floodwaters.** Any water that runs over from normal reservoirs, such as lakes, ponds, and streams, as a part of a flood.

**frostbite.** Damaged skin or tissue caused by exposure to extreme cold.

**geosynchronous satellite.** A human-made object in space that orbits the earth at a speed that equals the planet's rotation. This allows the satellite to stay over the same spot on the earth's surface.

**groundwater.** A reserve of water that is found in the spaces between soil particles and loose rock just below the ground.

**gust.** A short burst of very fast wind.

**heat exhaustion.** A medical condition caused by overexposure to heat. Symptoms include dizziness, a weak pulse, excessive sweating, headaches, and nausea.

**heat index.** A measure of heat that factors in the amount of humidity in the air to give you a better sense of how the temperature outdoors will really feel.

**heatstroke.** A life-threatening condition caused by the body overheating and being unable to cool off. Symptoms include extreme dizziness and nausea, a temperature of 104 degrees Fahrenheit, and hot, dry skin.

**high-pressure zone.** An area that has higher air pressure than areas around it.

**humidity.** A measurement of how much moisture is in the air.

**hydrologist.** A scientist who studies how water moves, reacts, and changes in all of its forms.

**hypothermia.** A life-threatening condition in which the body has cooled beyond its ability to maintain an internal temperature of 98.6 degrees Fahrenheit. Symptoms include clumsiness, confusion, and drowsiness.

**insulation.** A protective layer that prevents energy from traveling from one area to another.

**lift.** Something that causes the upward movement of air.

**meteorologist.** A scientist who studies the weather.

**minerals.** Naturally occurring substances that are not plant- or animal-based, and that are essential to the proper functioning of the body.

**negative charge.** A buildup of electrons that have become detached from atoms. The flow of electrons from a negatively charged object to a positively charged one creates an electrical current.

**observations.** Carefully collected data gathered by watching something closely.

**oxygen.** A chemical element that makes up about 20 percent of the earth's atmosphere and is necessary for animal life.

**polar-orbiting satellite.** A human-made object in space that travels around the earth, crossing over the North and South Poles in its orbit.

**positive charge.** The state of having lost electrons, so that an atom has more positively charged protons than negatively charged electrons.

**precipitation.** Water that falls to the ground in the form of rain, snow, hail, or sleet.

**reservoir.** A lake that is used to store water for later use.

**saturation point.** The point at which there is no longer room to add a substance, such as water, to a vapor, such as air.

**sea level.** The height of the oceans on earth. Sea level is the baseline from which all other altitude measurements are determined.

**temperature.** A measure of the amount of heat in the air. In the United States, temperature is measured in degrees Fahrenheit.

**thermal energy.** A type of energy that makes molecules move around. Thermal energy can be felt as heat.

**unstable.** In the atmosphere, having differences in temperature and pressure that are likely to create movement or changes in weather.

**updraft.** Air that is moving upward.

**vapor.** A loose cloud of molecules, also called a gas.

**weather balloon.** A hydrogen- or helium-filled balloon designed to carry weather instruments up through various layers of the atmosphere to measure weather conditions at different altitudes.

**wildland.** Area that has not been altered by human habitation.

# LEARN MORE

When you're ready to continue your weather adventure, you may want to jump online to visit some of the amazing weather resources there. All these websites provide up-to-date information about our changing world, and can be excellent places to start your exploration.

## CENTERS FOR DISEASE CONTROL AND PREVENTION (CDC)  cdc.gov/disasters

The CDC works to protect the public from potential threats to their health. Their disaster-preparedness website includes information to help people prepare for and avoid natural disasters.

## MOUNT WASHINGTON OBSERVATORY

*mountwashington.org*

On the top of Mount Washington in the White Mountains of New Hampshire, the Mount Washington Observatory experiences some of the most extreme weather on earth. Find out what it's like to live at a weather station through blog posts, webcams, and photo galleries on their website.

## NATIONAL AERONAUTICS AND SPACE ADMINISTRATION  nasa.gov

NASA is in charge of the space program in the United States. NASA satellites continually monitor the weather and climate from space. Their homepage is a great jumping-off point to learn more about NASA's programs and see some amazing photos. You may want to also visit some other NASA pages:

### SciJinks  scijinks.gov

A joint project created by NASA and NOAA, this site is all about the weather. It has useful information, games, and videos to help kids understand how weather works.

### The GRACE Project  nasa.gov/mission_pages/Grace

Find out more about the results of the GRACE mission to track aquifers around the world at the mission's homepage.

## NATIONAL INTERAGENCY FIRE CENTER (NIFC)

*nifc.gov*

The NIFC works to predict wildfires and manages resources so that personnel, equipment, and information reach areas that are battling wildland fires. Their website includes photos of wildfires, wildfire safety and prevention information, and updates on their mission and activities.

## NATIONAL OCEANOGRAPHIC AND ATMOSPHERIC ADMINISTRATION (NOAA)  noaa.gov

In the United States, NOAA studies the weather, climate, oceans, and coasts. A big part of that mission is working to predict weather events and to understand how those events are impacted by changes in the climate. In addition to their site at noaa.gov, NOAA oversees several weather-related programs with websites you may want to visit:

## NOAA Photo Library

flickr.com/photos/noaaphotolib

The NOAA photo library includes pictures taken by NOAA scientists on their research expeditions. You can find amazing photos of weather, scenery, and even ocean animals in their Flickr photostream.

## National Weather Service (NWS)  weather.gov

The NWS gathers weather data and provides forecasts for the entire country. On their site, you can enter your zip code for up-to-date forecasts and weather warnings in your area, and also search by date to find historical weather information.

## National Severe Storms Laboratory (NSSL)  nssl.noaa.gov

The NSSL focuses on predicting and lessening the danger from severe weather events such as blizzards, ice storms, flash floods, tornadoes, and lightning. Their website includes a great primer called "Severe Weather 101," as well as information on the VORTEX tornado projects.

## climate.gov

This website focuses on information related to climate. You can find recent climate news here, as well as information about how climate and global weather systems work.

## National Hurricane Center (NHC)  nhc.noaa.gov

The NHC tracks and predicts hurricane activity. Their site includes helpful tips on hurricane preparedness and safety, information on approaching storms, stories about historical storms, and hurricane statistics.

## NORTHWEST AVALANCHE CENTER (NWAC)  nwac.us

The NWAC works to prevent avalanche deaths by gathering data, forecasting conditions, and educating the public in avalanche zones throughout the American Northwest. A collaboration between the National Forest Service and a nonprofit group, their website includes forecasts and FAQs.

## UNITED STATES GEOLOGICAL SURVEY (USGS)

*usgs.gov*

The USGS gathers and studies scientific information about the earth, including water, energy, and mineral resources. Their website has information on earthquakes, volcanoes, water conditions, and landslides.

# PICTURE CREDITS/ ACKNOWLEDGMENTS

**All credits are listed clockwise from top left, unless otherwise noted.**

**Page 1:** Eric Ray Davidson/NBC/NBCU Photo Bank via Getty Images

**Page 2:** (left to right) NOAA, wanaapong/Shutterstock, Caleb Holder/Shutterstock, Irina Igumnova/Dreamstime

**Page 3:** Eric Ray Davidson/NBC/NBCU Photo Bank via Getty Images

**Pages 4-5:** Wanda Hartwigsen/NOAA's NWS Collection, Sean Waugh NOAA/NSSL/VORTEX II, NOAA, Sean Waugh NOAA/NSSL/VORTEX II, NOAA

**Page 6:** (top to bottom) NG Images/Alamy Stock Photo, Pictorial Press Ltd/Alamy Stock Photo, Peter Kramer/NBC/NBC NewsWire via Getty Images

**Page 7:** (top to bottom) Warships/Alamy Stock Photo, Warships/Alamy Stock Photo, Peter Kramer/NBC/NBC NewsWire via Getty Images

**Pages 8-9:** Lt. Mike Silah/NOAA, NOAA, NOAA/JMA/NESDIS Environmental Visualization Laboratory, VORTEX II, Reuters/Alamy Stock Photo

**Pages 10-11:** VORTEX II

**Pages 12-13:** Sean Waugh NOAA/NSSL, VORTEX II, NASA/JSC, VORTEX II, VORTEX II, NOAA/NSSL, VORTEX II, NOAA/NWS collection

**Pages 14-15:** NOAA Photo Library/OAR/ERL/NSSL, RGB Ventures/SuperStock/Alamy Stock Photo, Minerva Studio/Shutterstock, Neal Dorst/OAR/AOML/NOAA, OAR/ERL/Wave Propagation Laboratory/NOAA

**Page 16:** (top to bottom) Dave Chapman/Alamy Stock Photo, NOAA/NWS, Jonathan Weiss/Alamy Stock Photo

**Page 17:** (top to bottom) iStockphoto, suzutake/Shutterstock

**Pages 18-19:** Ryszard Stelmachowicz/Shutterstock, Dan Tautan/Shutterstock, VORTEX II, Tamara Hughbanks Harding/Dreamstime

**Pages 20-21:** Olaf Naami/Shutterstock, Shawn Smith/NOAA Weather in Focus Photo Contest 2015, NOAA, Alexey Kljatov/Shutterstock

**Page 22:** Ramon Berk/iStockphoto

**Page 23:** (top to bottom) NOAA, Library of Congress, George Grantham Bain Collection/Library of Congress

**Pages 24-25:** Sunny Forest/Shutterstock

**Pages 26-27:** David Greitze/Shutterstock, NASA, Piyaset/Shutterstock, Arthur Rothstein/Library of Congress

**Pages 28-29:** franckreporter/iStockphoto, mira/Alamy Stock Photo, NOAA, Pulsar Images/Alamy Stock Photo, Captain Albert E. Theberge/NOAA Corps, Westhoff/iStockphoto, Philip Allen McInroy/Stockimo/Alamy Stock Photo

**Pages 30-31:** Richard Ellis/Alamy Stock Photo, epa european pressphoto agency bv./Alamy Stock Photo, NOAA/NWS, gjohnstonphoto/iStockphoto, winstonwolf89/iStockphoto

**Pages 32-33:** A Kazantsev/Shutterstock, Ron Buskirk/Alamy Stock Photo, Christopher Penler/Alamy Live News, Alex Stepanov/iStockphoto

**Pages 34-35:** Lysogor/iStockphoto

**Pages 36-37:** Marty Bahamonde/FEMA, Leon Werdinger/Alamy Stock Photo, Marvin Nauman/FEMA News Photo, Jana Baldwin/FEMA News Photo, Lieut. Commander Mark Moran/NOAA Corps/NMAO/AOC, Lieut. Commander Mark Moran/NOAA Corps/NMAO/AOC, George Armstrong/FEMA News Photo

**Pages 38-39:** (all photos) National Interagency Fire Center

**Page 40:** (top to bottom) Mike Doukas/USGS, James G. Moore/USGS

**Page 41:** Terry Leighley/USGS, Leonid Plotkin/Alamy Stock Photo, USGS

**Pages 42-43:** med ved/iStockphoto, creativenrnage/iStockphoto, UpperCut Images/Alamy Stock Photo, Deepspacedave/iStockphoto, Dave Saville/FEMA News Photo, Design Pics Inc/Alamy Stock Photo

**Pages 44-45:** Minerva Studio/Shutterstock, NOAA

# CAPTAIN RAPTOR

## and the SPACE PIRATES

**KEVIN O'MALLEY** and **PATRICK O'BRIEN**

*Illustrations by* **PATRICK O'BRIEN**

**BLOOMSBURY**

NEW YORK  LONDON  OXFORD  NEW DELHI  SYDNEY

IN THE MISTY SKIES ABOVE THE PLANET JURASSICA, A *DARK AND SINISTER SHAPE* IS SEEN MOVING AMONG THE CLOUDS.

SUDDENLY . . .

BOOM!

A CANNON ROARS OVERHEAD.

AMID THE FIRE AND SMOKE, THE PIRATE SHIP *BLACKROT* DESCENDS TO THE GROUND.

THE HATCH FLIES OPEN, AND A *MOB OF MISSHAPEN MUTANTS* AND *REPTILIAN CYBORGS* FLOW LIKE A RIVER OUT OF THE SHIP, SCREAMING AND SHOUTING AND WAVING THEIR LASER SWORDS.

THE CITIZENS OF JURASSICA ARE IN A *PANIC* AS THE SPACE PIRATES RAID THE IMPERIAL PALACE.

*SMASHING* THROUGH A HEAVY DOOR, THE RAMPAGING ROGUES FIND THE FAMOUS *JEWELS OF JURASSICA.*

WEIGHED DOWN WITH TREASURE, THE PIRATES DASH BACK INTO THEIR SHIP AND BLAST OFF, LEAVING THE PALACE IN RUINS.

"THOSE PIRATES MUST BE STOPPED!" ROARS THE PRESIDENT.

"BUT SIR, WHAT CAN WE DO?"

"I'LL TELL YOU WHAT WE DO. WE CALL . . ."

THE STARSHIP *MEGATOOTH* IS PREPARED FOR BATTLE.

CAPTAIN RAPTOR ASSEMBLES HIS FEARLESS CREW:

PROFESSOR ANGLEOPTEROUS: MASTER ENGINEER.

SERGEANT BRICKTHOROUS: WEAPONS SPECIALIST.

LIEUTENANT THREETOE: ACE PILOT.

"OKAY CREW, *BUCKLE UP,*" SAYS CAPTAIN RAPTOR. "LET'S TEACH THOSE HOOLIGANS A LESSON THEY WON'T FORGET! *3...2...1...*"

CAPTAIN RAPTOR'S TRUSTY PILOT, LIEUTENANT THREETOE, IS AT THE CONTROLS AS THE *MEGATOOTH RACES THROUGH SPACE*, FOLLOWING THE *BLACKROT'S* ION TRAIL.

THROUGH THE STAR CLUSTER OF REPTILIUS 4, FAR AROUND THE PERILUS NEBULA, THE *MEGATOOTH* CHASES THE FLEEING PIRATES.

AT LAST, CAPTAIN RAPTOR SPOTS THE *BLACKROT*, DRIFTING WITHOUT POWER NEAR A SMALL, UNKNOWN MOON.

"CAPTAIN," SAYS THREETOE, "SEE THAT SMOKE? THEIR SHIP IS DAMAGED. *NOW'S OUR CHANCE! I'M GOING IN!*"

"NO, *PULL BACK*, THREETOE. *I SMELL A TRAP!*"

CAPTAIN RAPTOR AND HIS CREW GO *SPINNING UNCONTROLLABLY* TOWARD THE ROCKY MOON.

COULD THIS BE *THE END* OF CAPTAIN RAPTOR?

AT THE LAST MOMENT, CAPTAIN RAPTOR AND BRICKTHOROUS MANAGE TO CONTROL THE SPIN AND GET HER NOSE UP. THE *MEGATOOTH* HITS **HARD**, THEN SCRAPES AND SLIDES TO A STOP.

THE CAPTAIN AND CREW STAGGER OUT ONTO A BARREN LANDSCAPE.

"STRANGE, THIS MOON DOESN'T SHOW UP ON ANY OF MY SPACE MAPS. AND IT SEEMS TO BE COMPLETELY DESERTED."

ANGLEOPTEROUS EXAMINES THE SHIP'S ENGINES. "CAPTAIN, OUR PLUTONIC SERVOSCOPE IS SHATTERED. THERE'S NO WAY TO FIX IT—WE DON'T HAVE THE PARTS. I'M AFRAID WE'RE STUCK HERE."

"WE'LL GET OFF THIS ROCK, OR MY NAME ISN'T CAPTAIN RAP—" SUDDENLY, CAPTAIN RAPTOR *SPRINGS UP* AND RUSHES OFF INTO THE BUSHES.

HE RETURNS, DRAGGING A WRETCHED CREATURE IN RAGGED CLOTHES.

"I CAUGHT THIS SCOUNDREL SPYING ON US!"

"WHAT ARE YOU DOING HERE?" DEMANDS CAPTAIN RAPTOR.

"AH, SIR, I WAS JUST GETTIN' READY TA ASK *YOU* THE SAME THING."

"*I* AM CAPTAIN RAPTOR OF THE PLANET JURASSICA. NOW, WHO ARE YOU?"

"ME NAME? WHY, IT'S BLOODY BART SCALA—ER, UH—IT'S BART SCALAWAG, SIR. AND 'TWAS A BAND OF *ROTTEN PIRATES* THAT DONE IT, CAP'N. CAPTURED ME SHIP AND LEFT ME HERE, THE SCURVY DOGS. LEFT ME *MAROONED* ON THIS MISERABLE PLANET."

"BUT I SEE YER IN A SPOT OF TROUBLE. LOOKS LIKE YER SHIP'S SEEN BETTER DAYS. YA MIGHT BE NEEDIN' A BIT OF MY HANDIWORK, THEN?"

"I DOUBT IT. NOT UNLESS YOU'VE GOT A NEW PLUTONIC SERVOSCOPE UNDER THAT CAPE."

"WHY, I CAN RIG UP THAT OLD BARGE OF YERS AND HAVE HER ALL SHIPSHAPE IN NO TIME, CAP'N. BUT YOU'LL HAVE TO BE TAKIN' ME WITH YA WHEN YA BLAST OUT OF HERE."

CAPTAIN RAPTOR STARES INTO SCALAWAG'S BEADY EYES, THEN SAYS, "VERY WELL."

"PUT YER TRUST IN ME, CAP'N. YOU WON'T REGRET IT."

TRUE TO HIS WORD, SCALAWAG REPAIRS THE BROKEN SHIP.

"NOW, THREETOE," SAYS CAPTAIN RAPTOR, "*LET'S GET THIS BIRD IN THE AIR.*"

THE *MEGATOOTH* SLOWLY LIFTS OFF THE GROUND.

"CAP'N," SAYS SCALAWAG, "I RECKON THOSE RAPSCALLIONS HAVE HEADED BACK TO JURASSICA. THERE'S STILL MORE TREASURE TO BE FOUND THERE.

AND WITH YOU OUT OF THE WAY, THERE'D BE NO STOPPING THEM.

IF I WAS A PIRATE, THAT'S WHAT I'D DO.

AND MAY I SAY, SIR, THAT IF YOU WAS TO FLY RIGHT THROUGH THE PERILUS NEBULA, YOU'D GET TO JURASSICA TWICE AS FAST."

"THAT'S RISKY, SCALAWAG. MANY SHIPS HAVE GONE INTO THE NEBULA, BUT FEW HAVE COME OUT.

BUT JURASSICA NEEDS US. WE'LL HAVE TO TAKE THE CHANCE. THREETOE, *TAKE US IN.*"

THE *MEGATOOTH* ENTERS THE NEBULA, A MYSTERIOUS CLOUD OF GAS AND COSMIC DUST.

"THIS PLACE GIVES ME THE CREEPS, CAPTAIN," SAYS THREETOE.

"HOLD IT TOGETHER, MAN. YOU CAN DO THIS. STEADY ON," SAYS CAPTAIN RAPTOR.

"*LOOK OUT!*" YELLS SCALAWAG. "*HERE COMES TROUBLE!*"

COULD *THIS* BE THE END OF CAPTAIN RAPTOR?

"*CAP'N!*" SHOUTS SCALAWAG. "I'VE TANGLED WITH THIS MONSTER BEFORE. IF YOU CAN GET TO THE ELECTRIC PANEL ON ITS NECK, YOU CAN CUT ITS POWER LINE. THAT'S *THE ONLY WAY* TO DEFEAT IT!"

CAPTAIN RAPTOR CLIMBS OUT THE HATCH, *LEAPS* ONTO THE ROBOKRON'S BACK, AND CLAMBERS UP TO ITS NECK. OPENING THE ELECTRIC PANEL, HE SEES DOZENS OF WIRES. *WHICH ONE TO CUT?*

WITH THE ROBOKRON'S TEETH SLOWLY *CRUSHING* THE MEGATOOTH, CAPTAIN RAPTOR REACHES IN AND *YANKS OUT* EVERYTHING HE SEES.

THERE'S A *SHOWER OF SPARKS*, AND THEN A *HUGE ELECTRIC JOLT* HURTLES HIM BACK ONTO THE MEGATOOTH.

THE ROBOKRON GOES LIMP AND BEGINS TO FALL JUST AS CAPTAIN RAPTOR *DIVES* INTO THE *MEGATOOTH'S* HATCH.

"*STEP ON IT, THREETOE!* LET'S SEE WHAT THIS SHIP CAN DO!"

THE *MEGATOOTH ZOOMS* OUT FROM BELOW THE FALLING MONSTER, THEN *SPEEDS* BACK THROUGH SPACE TO JURASSICA.

ARRIVING IN THE SKIES ABOVE JURASSICA, THE *MEGATOOTH* LIES IN WAIT.

BRICKTHOROUS CHARGES UP THE BLASTOCANNONS. "*READY FOR BATTLE*, CAPTAIN," HE REPORTS.

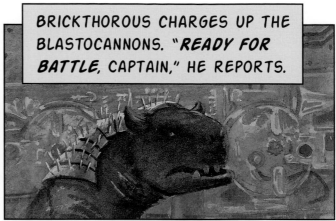

SOON, THE PIRATE SHIP EMERGES FROM THE MISTS.

"*FIRE!*" YELLS CAPTAIN RAPTOR. *THE BATTLE IS ON!*

CAPTAIN RAPTOR TURNS TO SHOUT AN ORDER AT SCALAWAG, BUT NO ONE IS THERE. "NOW WHERE'D THAT RASCAL GO?"

JUST THEN HE SEES THE *MEGATOOTH'S* SHUTTLE CRAFT LEAVING THE SHIP, WITH *BART SCALAWAG* GRINNING AT THE CONTROLS.

SCALAWAG TURNS ON THE RADIO COMMUNICATOR AND SHOUTS AT THE PIRATES, "*LET ME THROUGH, YA SCURVY DOGS!* BLOODY BART SCALAWAG HAS RETURNED! AND YOU'LL NOT GET RID O' ME THIS TIME!"

THROUGH A *HAIL OF CANNON FIRE,* THE SHUTTLE CRAFT MAKES ITS WAY TO THE PIRATE SHIP AND GLIDES INSIDE.

"WE CAN'T TAKE MUCH MORE OF THIS," SHOUTS THREETOE. "THE BLACKROT'S TOO BIG FOR US. WE'RE SHOT FULL OF HOLES!"

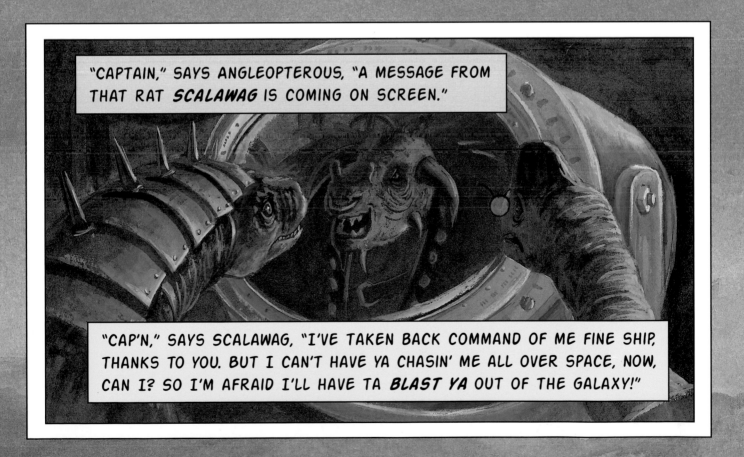

"CAPTAIN," SAYS ANGLEOPTEROUS, "A MESSAGE FROM THAT RAT **SCALAWAG** IS COMING ON SCREEN."

"CAP'N," SAYS SCALAWAG, "I'VE TAKEN BACK COMMAND OF ME FINE SHIP, THANKS TO YOU. BUT I CAN'T HAVE YA CHASIN' ME ALL OVER SPACE, NOW, CAN I? SO I'M AFRAID I'LL HAVE TA **BLAST YA** OUT OF THE GALAXY!"

IS **THIS** THE END OF CAPTAIN RAPTOR?

"CAPTAIN, *WE'RE DONE FOR!*"

"RELAX, THREETOE. I NEVER REALLY TRUSTED SCALAWAG. SO BEFORE THE BATTLE I PACKED A SMALL *GOING-AWAY PRESENT* INTO OUR SHUTTLE CRAFT. I THINK THAT SCALAWAG WILL FIND IT QUITE . . . EXPLOSIVE."

"IF YOU WOULD KINDLY PUSH THIS RED BUTTON . . ."

"IT WOULD BE *MY PLEASURE*, CAPTAIN."

THE BACK OF THE *BLACKROT* IS TAKEN OFF BY THE EXPLOSION. THE SHIP *SPIRALS* DOWN TO THE PLANET BELOW.

THE PIRATES TUMBLE OUT, DAZED AND DEFEATED. TONS OF TREASURE SPILL ONTO THE GROUND.

THE DINOSAURS OF JURASSICA CAN REST EASY NOW. CAPTAIN RAPTOR AND HIS FEARLESS CREW HAVE **SAVED THE DAY** AGAIN.

"SCALAWAG, YOU'VE LOST YOUR SHIP AGAIN. BUT THIS TIME YOU WON'T BE LEFT ALL ALONE ON A DESERT PLANET. YOU'LL BE SPENDING PLENTY OF TIME WITH YOUR CREW—*IN PRISON.*"

FIRST PUBLISHED IN THE UNITED STATES OF AMERICA IN SEPTEMBER 2007
BY WALKER BOOKS FOR YOUNG READERS, AN IMPRINT OF BLOOMSBURY PUBLISHING, INC.
WWW.BLOOMSBURY.COM

BLOOMSBURY IS A REGISTERED TRADEMARK OF BLOOMSBURY PUBLISHING PLC

FOR INFORMATION ABOUT PERMISSION TO REPRODUCE SELECTIONS FROM THIS BOOK, WRITE TO
PERMISSIONS, BLOOMSBURY CHILDREN'S BOOKS, 1385 BROADWAY, NEW YORK, NEW YORK 10018
BLOOMSBURY BOOKS MAY BE PURCHASED FOR BUSINESS OR PROMOTIONAL USE. FOR INFORMATION ON BULK
PURCHASES PLEASE CONTACT MACMILLAN CORPORATE AND PREMIUM SALES DEPARTMENT AT
SPECIALMARKETS@MACMILLAN.COM

LIBRARY OF CONGRESS CATALOGING-IN-PUBLICATION DATA
O'MALLEY, KEVIN.
CAPTAIN RAPTOR AND THE SPACE PIRATES / KEVIN O'MALLEY AND PATRICK O'BRIEN ;
ILLUSTRATIONS BY PATRICK O'BRIEN.
P.     CM.
SUMMARY: CAPTAIN RAPTOR AND THE CREW OF THE *MEGATOOTH* ARE CALLED BACK INTO
ACTION TO SAVE THE PLANET JURASSICA FROM ROGUE SPACE PIRATES.
ISBN-13: 978-0-8027-9571-7 • ISBN-10: 0-8027-9571-4 (HARDCOVER)
ISBN-13: 978-0-8027-9572-4 • ISBN-10: 0-8027-9572-2 (REINFORCED)
[1. DINOSAURS–FICTION. 2. PIRATES–FICTION. 3. SCIENCE FICTION.] I. O'BRIEN, PATRICK, ILL. II. TITLE.
PZ7.O526CSP 2007          [E]–DC22          2006101182

ILLUSTRATIONS CREATED WITH WATERCOLOR AND GOUACHE
TYPESET IN ACTION MAN
BOOK DESIGN BY PATRICK O'BRIEN
PRINTED IN CHINA BY C&C OFFSET PRINTING CO., LTD., SHENZHEN, GUANGDONG
6 8 10 9 7 5